OUR
INVISIBLE
WALL

Improve your relationships
by understanding our
hidden emotions

by Tove Frisvold
Psychoanalytical Psychotherapist
Institute of Psychotherapy and Social Studies

SESHAT PRESS

With gratitude to my family, friends, and all I learned from my clients!

We are born with emotions.
We are born with feelings.
But nobody taught us how to handle them.

ISBN: 978-1-9163041-1-6

SESHAT PRESS
An imprint of Northern Bridge Productions
Charity No. 1077637
Enquiries: seshat@amberbridge.co.uk

CONTENTS

CHAPTER 1

What is the Wall?

WHAT HAPPENS IF YOU are in a relationship with a person who is never in the wrong?

It can be a partner, a family member, a friend, somebody you work with, and this person is incapable of admitting to the point of being in denial.

He or she often blames you and it seems for them there is no other way to behave.

One of my clients, a married woman in her forties said: "I would do anything for this relationship except leave".

Sometimes her partner was charming and seemingly attentive and at other times, he was withdrawn, even angry and if asked why, he came with some reason to criticise her. It never occurred to him that he could ever play a role in what could become a conflict between them, as it was never his fault.

He seemed stuck in denial. If confronted with his own behaviour he was never in the wrong. Why? She asked the question and so did I.

Could a loving partner stay with somebody who too often would criticise or not be able to listen or take any correction, even suggestion?

The client felt the pain each time he blamed her and she avoided the pain by thinking his behaviour might change or something might hopefully change, one day, if she tried hard enough.

As this came up as a prime pattern in couples that came to see me, I started to make a "system", a methodology for this behaviour.

I perceived it as an almost invisible structure that keeps a person's emotions undisclosed. I found that this pattern of behaviour, described by Freud as defence mechanisms, shows a person who cant deal with emotions and hides behind this "system", which I started to recognise as a Wall. At the same time these people could present a fairly normal persona especially to newcomers. So, the woman, the client was puzzled by the existence of this barrier, which was displayed mainly by denial and blame, forming almost an actual shape of an obstacle between them.

Why would her husband who seemed to have a good life need a wall? He denied any such block.

What happens between these two people? What can be done about it? First accept that he, or she, has built this defence to avoid dealing with painful emotions.

How can their relationship become sufficiently fluid for the structure to become diminished and less painful.

Living with a person behind the Wall can cause distress, grief, and pain. In other couples there could be different symptoms, but the core problem is the same. Often it appears because the one behind the wall, the Wall-Hider will not admit the situation exists. If pinned down he or she has a variety of reasons for why the defence mechanisms are in place.

As another client said:

> "In my experience living with someone such as this results in a slow, insidious loss of energy, confidence, and self-respect. Remember that line in the movie *Pretty Woman*, when Julia Roberts says to Richard Gere that if 'people put you down enough, you start to believe it?'
>
> It can take a long time to realize you are losing your personal power, but if your opinion is never accounted for, if you feel that your voice is not heard, or that you are never validated as a person you can start to doubt your own self-worth."

The concept of the wall can be used as a model to understand the behaviour of the person next to us, a partner, a boss, somebody close to us with an incapacity to admit or even see themselves. This resistance can be both frustrating and detrimental to the other's life and wellbeing.

It is not a matter of social class or creed, these individuals can be on any level, in organisations, the staff-room, corporate.

So let us examine this behaviour and where it stems from, and seek the possibility for the recipient to find his or her own place, by using tools and ways which will eventually empower when dealing with such a person as the Wall-Hider.

Instead of reacting and fighting we can explore the way to acceptance, even freeing up from the bondage. Also for the Wall-Hider to find some point of recognition.

CHAPTER 2

Who is Behind The Wall?

SO WHAT HAPPENS WHEN two people in a couple are operating from different sides of The Wall and what can be done about it?

Many of us are exhausted, exasperated, frustrated and unhappy living with or close to somebody who is emotionally trapped and hiding behind their own defence mechanisms. When did this start and why?

First the client might benefit from discovering a structure which has been described earlier as a shape resembling a Wall.

This image can help to clarify what the client finds difficult in the partner and why it is perceived as painful when communication is not received, in the way expected.

The Wall, unhealthy, sometimes dangerous, constructed to keep one safely distant from others. In spite of the significant role our emotions and feelings play we have not learned how to handle or manage them. Depending on formative years and what has been shown to us in our family, we become emotionally coherent or we don't.

Most likely a person who has not had a secure enough childhood to develop emotions in a healthy way starts automatically to build defences.

And possibly they've spent their first years in a family that felt unsafe, for example a chastising and angry mother, a strict and punishing father, insensitive to the child's needs. This might have lead to this intuitive building of defences, based on protection against expectation of being hurt or even attacked.

In the majority of cases the Wall-Hider does not respond to emotions. He or she is not aligned to others feelings so when we come close to them, express an emotion of any kind they are not able to respond, mirror or even acknowledge what we shared or expressed. Instead they have ways of not "tuning in" to the other. They can quickly come with a rational solution or deflect by changing the subject or even use blame.

IN THERAPY:

How is the wife mentioned earlier managing their relationship? She has tried relentlessly to get a satisfying response and finally exhausted and defeated even blamed herself for the failure. What is wrong with me? What am I doing that is not right? The client's emotional life gets no nourishment and she wonders how much more she can take?

She and I decided to explore what it would be like if she left the relationship We also looked at what needed to change for her to stay?

She never thought her emotions needed an examination as

they had always been a natural part of her. Neither did she think her behaviour needed any adapting, surely it was part of the authentic her. "I imagined we would be talking about my husband's behaviour. That's why I'm here."

When researching for this book I was surprised how many relationships suffered from this dynamic. Most of these people thought they were trapped in a unique and isolated situation and had no idea many others had the same challenges.

Let's examine this behaviour and explore where it stems from to see how we can transform the pain and suffering of the recipient. We will look at the tools that can empower.

In life we may not have learned how to handle or manage these emotions and feelings, depending on our individual experience of our families, genes and the examples we have been given growing up. Whether or not we become emotionally coherent or not seems to be dependent on our life experiences in our formative years.

- **The Client** – this is the person who seeks help to improve the relationship.

- **The Wall Hider** – this is the person who is hiding behind The Wall.

- **The Wall** – the structure that impedes effective communication and provides safety and distance from others.

As already mentioned, in the majority of cases The Wall Hider doesn't respond to emotions. He or she is not able to respond effectively to the feelings of others. This means that when we are close to them and express emotion of any kind, they are not capable of responding or mirroring.

The recipient has tried relentlessly to get a satisfying

response and finally (exhausted and defeated) blame themselves for the failure. They might question themselves: What is wrong with me? What am I doing wrong? Why has my partner become unable to ever admit fault, and why does he/she always blame me? In these situations, the emotional life of the person before The Wall receives no nourishment, and they wonder how much more they can take.

.

WHY EMOTIONS MATTER

The client, the wife, agreed to explore what it would be like if she left the relationship. We also looked at what needed to change for her to stay. She knew changes had to happen so she could find a way to save herself.

We are born with emotions.
We are born with feelings.
But nobody taught us how to handle them.

Let's look at that last sentence. ". . . nobody taught us how to handle them." So, why hasn't this happened? The consequence seems to be that "we simply don't know how to handle them".

Emotions are like a secret room full of treasure that is seldom opened. We are all born with them, we all know they are there, but as they have never been adequately recognised we have not been given any "instructions" on how to manage them. In many families, emotions are discouraged and considered a sign of weakness.

CHAPTER 3

Why Emotions Matter

ANTONIO DAMASIO, THE American/Portuguese neuroscientist has produced research in neuroscience showing that emotions play a central role in social cognition and decision making. In his book *Descarte's Error* he writes:

"Why are feelings important? Feelings connect us with all living beings and with our surroundings. They propel and drive us through life. They tell us who we are. If our relationship with our own emotions is not good, we can't see our own reality clearly, and will have difficulties relating to others. The consequence of this is that the most rewarding of all existing feelings – love – will be difficult to 'construct'."

As Melody Beattie says in her book *Codependent No More*:

"Our feelings can provide us with clues to ourselves, our desires, wants and ambitions. They help us discover ourselves, what we really think. Our emotions also tap into the deep part of us that seeks and knows truth and desires self-preservation, self-enhancement, safety and goodness. Our emotions are connected to our conscious, cognitive-thought process and the mysterious gifts called instinct and intuition."

As a young client, addicted to alcohol, later said during his recovery: "My trouble was that I had no emotions, even when drunk. Reasoning was another thing because I could believe in that. People used to say: 'You're a hard one to know. I can never tell what you're feeling.'"

By starting working on the perception that he had a wall and what he could do to try to dismantle it, he began to have a sense of emotional existence.

This happened in tandem with his going to Alcoholics Anonymous meetings, where he had the opportunity to share his feelings with strangers. After a few months, he came back to me and said: "Now I feel much more connected, both with myself and others. I can even feel empathy, and last week I even called somebody in my main group and asked if he was ok which has never happened before!"

Emotions do not show up in the language of school reports, performance reviews or application results. Our society, the whole western world as we know it, is based on achievements, grades and results. According to Marcia Reynolds in her book *How To Outsmart Your Brain*, our education system is based purely on the rational.

As Robert Burney (*The Dance of the Wounded Souls*) says:

"Our civilisation has been out of balance towards the left brain way of thinking – what you see is all there is, concrete rational. Perhaps in reaction to earlier times of being out of balance the other way, superstition and ignorance. Because emotional energy can not be seen or measured or weighed ("the x-ray shows you've got 5 pounds of grief in there") emotions were discounted and devalued." He goes on to say most of us grew up in a society that taught us that being too emotional was a bad thing that we should avoid.

In some families, feelings don't count, feelings are somehow wrong."

Melody Beattie says in her book, *Codependent No More*:

"As they are not listened to, the family member ceases relating to them. It may appear easier, at times, not to feel. Instead we try to make our feelings disappear. To acknowledge how we really feel would demand a decision, action, or change on our part. It would bring us face-to-face with reality. We would become aware of what we were thinking, what we want, and what we need to do. And we are not ready to do that yet."

IN THERAPY:

To begin with we looked at how the wife, the client ended up in the relationship.

It always starts with attraction, and many people who exist behind walls compensate in various ways. They can be charming and debonair, even charismatic and magnetic. They invariably exhibit qualities that beguile. The relationship starts in much the same way as any other, but with time the client discovers there is an existing pattern that is detrimental. By this time, they are lost in the relationship, deeply ensconced and unable to walk away.

Occasionally there can be not just one but two Wall Hiders in a relationship. Their children who have taken up the pain of having two parents with a weakness, or inability to admit, and who therefore constantly attribute blame, can lead to a child becoming anxious and frequently ill.

But for the moment let's focus on the Client who suffers and The Wall Hider who seems unable to change their ingrained pattern of behaviour.

THE WORSHIP OF REASON

In the latter part of 1700s, William Blake started to question through poems and paintings the depths of what Freud called the subconscious underworld of awareness, in his quest to be a spiritual explorer.

Blake said that the English were terrified of their emotions and labelled this fear: URIZEN (You Reason). He said it was the ultimate incarnation of the British disease, an excessive worship of reason, which was often expressed in tyrannical fatherhood and arbitrary authority.

Blake was concerned about the 'blindness of feelings'. The repercussions for this obliterating of emotions can be overwhelming and can have a detrimental effect on our personal lives, family, school, the workplace and even on relationships between countries.

CHAPTER 4

Who Am I?

WHEN IT COMES TO handling emotions, we have grown up in a culture that has dismissed the need to understand them. We have created a society that is primarily based on valuing, encouraging and rewarding technical and rational achievements in schools, universities, organisations etc. But how can we be taught about emotions we don't even know we have?

In her book, *Daring Greatly – The Courage to be Vulnerable*, Brene Brown says:

"Our reluctance of "meeting" with dark emotions like fear, shame, grief, sadness, disappointment, guilt and shame are obvious – but on the other hand: to foreclose on our emotional life out of fear that the cost will be too high is to walk away from the very thing that gives purpose and meaning to living.

To simplify a system to discover WHO AM I? it was easier to introduce to clients that we could be pre-conditioned, and that our journeys begin in the same place (the family into which we were born). We seem to be a product of our mother's genes, our father's genes, our mother's behaviour, our father's behaviour, the relationship between them and their relationship with us."

Our detective work starts with The Family Map. This is the point at which we start to understand that every family member has played a role in what we have become: how we feel, how we behave and which behaviours don't serve us anymore, alongside the impact of our own behaviours on the people around us. We build internal totems of what good and bad feelings are. We learn from an early age, when we start socialising, those emotions that it's acceptable to express and those which need to be suppressed and repressed.

IN THERAPY:

The woman in the original couple I referenced was presented with The Family Map. I asked her to fill in the blanks with descriptions of the different family members and their distinctive character traits. Some of what this revealed surprised her. The interaction between her mother and father seemed quite similar to the relationship between her and her husband. I felt it important to emphasis the notion of "Who Am I?" to strengthen her insight into her capabilities, her positive strengths that have previously been unavailable to her.

As we worked on the descriptions of her mother, her father and their parents, the client was taken aback when

I called her "a product" of that family map. We spent time seeing where the character traits of each member interwove into her present personality.

Believing she was an individual, self-made, she was surprised at how many sides of her character she found she had inherited. So what did this mean for her? What did she need to do and how did her own relationship relate to her husband?

After going through each of the members in her family, she was quite clear when I asked which of these character traits had filtered down to her. She said: "It's so amazing! I never realised that I behave so much like my mother."

According to Andrea Brandt, in her article in *Psychology Today*: "If children don't create a new internal map as they grow up, their old way of interpreting the world can damage their ability to function as adults."

I showed this to my client and she seemed to understand this as an opportunity for both her and her husband to look at the possibility of changing some of the behaviour between them that had been so hurtful.

OUR LEARNED BEHAVIOUR

In his book *Codependence: The Dance of Wounded Souls*, the author Robert Burney:

> "We learned to have a dysfunctional relationship with self, with other people, and with life in early childhood. It is vital to start looking at ourselves and life from a whole new perspective, with different eyes. In order to do that, it is necessary to start being honest with our self. The first step is to admit to ourselves that we need help, in order to see our reality with more clarity so that we can start

changing our relationships and the way we define our needs in life. Only then can we unlearn old behaviour and start to discover a new way towards developing healthy relationships with self and others."

How do we get started on our journey once we have admitted to ourselves that we need help?

A good starting point is to draw a time-line from birth to the present indicating where life changes such as loss and hurt occurred and then you can acknowledge situations that shaped your life, relationships, good and bad. Only then can you start to make sense of your present.

We all have wounds from our childhood that depend on several factors, not only from our family, but also from the society in which we were brought up, or the community of which we were part of.

Sogyal Rinpoche tells us in *The Tibetan Book of Living and Dying*:

"We are fragmented into so many different aspects. We don't know who we really are, or what aspects of ourselves we should identify with or believe in. So many contradictory voices, dictates, and feelings fight for control over our inner lives that we find ourselves scattered everywhere, in all directions, leaving nobody at home. Meditation, then, is bringing the mind home."

THE FAMILY MAP

Through years of working with clients I have learnt that when they fill out their Family Map they come to see themselves as a 'product' of the family they are born into and grew up with. It is only then that they get a sense of "I" and "Who am I?"

What is also important is to see their partner's map in order to understand their pattern. It is then that the differences in how their families function becomes apparent.

In doing this both parties become aware of their parents, grandparents, their character traits and behaviour (both inherited and behavioural). This helps them to see which traits they have inherited and which behaviours they have been conditioned to take on.

There are six factors I have noticed that seem to influence and affect our behaviour:

1/. Mother's genes
2/. Father's genes
3/. Mother's behaviour
4/. Father's behaviour
5/. The relationship between them
6/. Their behaviour to us

When we study The Family Map (see diagram overleaf), we start discovering who we are, and realise why we behave the way we do. We start to see what character traits and behaviours have impacted us, and we might even go to a place which we call "ourself." – I, the product.

EMOTIONAL HONESTY

The value of this discovery is that we can then start to integrate the past into who we are today and begin our journey towards true understanding. From this point, we can move to self-acceptance.

Slowly we start to notice which behaviours don't serve us anymore. At first we might be in denial or feel a deep resistance

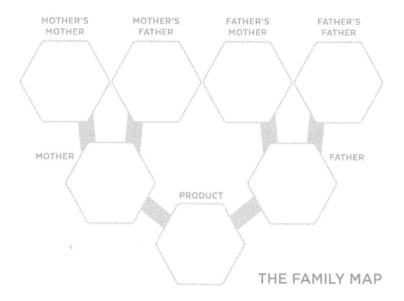

MOTHER'S MOTHER   MOTHER'S FATHER   FATHER'S MOTHER   FATHER'S FATHER

MOTHER   FATHER

PRODUCT

THE FAMILY MAP

while we go through this process, as it might cause fear and pain. Eventually, however, we will start to realise the value of accepting our inherited behaviour and how it might have hindered us having healthy relationships.

Eventually we arrive at a point where we have a choice to change our behaviour or go back to our old ways. If change is perceived as being too painful, we automatically start to build some resistance against the fear and pain of going through the process of transformation to get to know ourselves.

Acclaimed psychotherapist Susie Orbach says in her *Therapy Session* – Radio 3:

"One cannot discard one's past, like an unwanted coat. We have history, we come from somewhere, and we have attachments. Many are abused, ignored or hurt, and all those who might wish to flee and reinvent themselves, know they can only move forward with the acknowledgement of their past and what they've come from. Otherwise self-invention means dislocation from history and a deep dislocation from oneself. In striving to be the person that you want to be there may be enormous losses, fracturing and alienation."

The psychologist Abraham Maslow describes this passage as a time for self-actualization: "One can choose to go back toward safety or forward towards growth. Growth must be chosen again and again; fear must be overcome again and again."

When we embark on a journey towards change and choose the path of growth, we become resilient and better at understanding our emotions. From this vantage point we are better able to deal with partners who might have the defensive behaviours of The Wall Hider that has caused so much frustration and pain.

As we begin to shed old patterns of behaviour that no longer serve us, we can start to rebuild and improve our life.

IN THERAPY:

The wife, when filling out the descriptions, acknowledged her mother was obsessive and determined, and at the same time gave the impression of "living for others". In the description of her father she had written: "Scared, protective, loving, hardworking."

It was not a surprise when she discovered she, in turn, had put others first and spent a lot of energy trying to disguise scared feelings. She studied the character traits of all the family members and summed up for herself that she had inherited the qualities of living for others, determination and not giving up from her Mother, and her scared, protective, hardworking side from father. The price she was paying for harbouring some of these traits was her loss of freedom. In some cases, it was the people on the periphery during their upbringing who were more important than the core family members.

So how could the woman utilise this deeper knowledge of herself to her benefit?

More investigation in the following sessions enabled her to clear her life of what was not useful, and strengthen the aspects she had inherited that were positive. Would this be enough to improve her relationship with her partner? When I questioned her, she suddenly looked pale and upset and said:

"I sometimes feel I am missing out on an emotional connection that I have to accept I will never get. But the risk to leave for an eventual man who can match my passion and love for life is a risk I am not willing to take. The security I have now is too important." Then she decided it was time for her husband to join her in a session. She made it a condition of their continuing the relationship that he had therapy but he was reluctant and agreed only when I suggested he could see me alone.

We started our session with him recounting and explaining his childhood. It seemed that from an early age he saw things through rose-tinted glasses. When I asked him about his school years, he responded: "Nothing wrong with them." When asked about The Family Map and the characteristics of his parents he said they were: "Nothing to do with me." He was firmly behind The Wall, but what had put him there?

By examining his past, I saw these cut and dried responses were ways of keeping me and others at bay He worked in property and at 42 was hoping to start his own business. His wife had a career in marketing and was doing well. They were married with two children.

His responses and behaviour triggered questions in me. What part did he play in the situation/conflict of their relationship? Did he have any idea how his behaviour affected his wife? I was glad he agreed, albeit reluctantly, to come back for another session the following week.

IN THERAPY:

The husband opened our next session by focusing on his wife. I was surprised by how charming he was. For a moment, I almost began to doubt his wife, who had been my client for a long time. I was amazed by how well he played his role. He started to deflect me by telling stories from his village. It took me half a session to understand that this was part of his armour, and all the stories had been well rehearsed. He took me further away from the partnership by then elaborating on aspects of his job. He seemed to give in, by admitting he was worried about losing it.

As it was important for me to build up a connection with him I gave him some guidance on the work matter. It was a complex situation. He left without mentioning the intended reason for his visit – his wife. I felt he was pleased that once again he had kept me at bay. At the same time, however, we had made a positive connection.

The next session was about his work again. We touched on issues with his boss who he called stupid. He commented that his wife wasn't interested in his problems and had even dared to ask him whether he might have upset his boss. "She knew it was not my fault," he declared. This helped me to see how he avoided looking at his role in his own story.

ADDICTIVE RELATIONSHIPS

When we are able to ascertain the issues by moving to understand the situation better, self-therapy can start. We can pursue a healthier control of our emotions and act accordingly.

A helpful way of progressing to emotional recovery can be:

1/.   Discover the issue.
2/.   Own it and admit it.
3/.   Resolve it.

When we are incapable of being emotionally in touch, we continue to get into situations and into relationships with people that feel familiar to where we come from in terms of energy. This is a term that has been called "habit energies" by the Czech therapist and philosopher Garbo Mate.

As long as we continue this behaviour we are our own worst enemies. Discovering and developing awareness of our past wounds is the first step towards our emotional healing process.

This awareness begins with admittance. As long as we keep playing out old traumas from childhood and reacting unconsciously to situations and others, we are not capable of seeing clearly what is going on and our role in it.

The challenge is to not let the blame of others impact our field of pain when they put us down and make us feel not good enough. When our life is being dictated by the past, we keep on repeating and reacting to old emotional wounds. When we recognise this, we can begin to open up and "own" the wounds and eventually take responsibility for our part in what is happening. Only then can we change the way we experience life and finally resolve it.

IN THERAPY:

When the client's husband came to see me the next time there was an easier atmosphere between us and therefore he willingly filled out his Family Map. I felt this was because I was now concentrating more on him and his work and that he felt secure that there was nothing for me to find. His father was an engineer and his mother was a housewife. They had a calm relationship and seldom or never had an exchange of or about emotions.

When the whole map was filled out he sat in silence and looked at each bubble and mumbled: "My wife always complains that I don't do emotions!"

ATTACHMENT IN RELATIONSHIPS

A huge challenge many couples face in their relationship is how to find the right "attachment" with an ability to be both close and separate. Based on our family programming, we might feel incomplete or unable to cope without the other person's presence in our life, or we might not be able to cope with constant closeness and prefer to continue much the same life we led before we got married and so retain our independence.

People are often not aware they're enacting preconditioned behaviours. It's here that it becomes important that a couple finds a way to understand their differing needs and where those needs stem from.

Daniel J. Siege in his book: *The Developing Mind* emphasis the importance in childhood to be "felt" by the parent, and later in life with the therapist. This is dependent on the parents' sensitivity to signals and is the essence of secure attachments. It can inform us how two people "being" with each other permits emotional communication and a sense of connection to be established at any age.

Because we have not been taught how to deal with our emotions or have not even acknowledge that we have them, we were brought up with certain beliefs, ideals or myths about relationships, and how we should live and be in a family. To sum up therefore, the main role models, although we may not like it, seem to be the "family unit".

UNHEALTHY BEHAVIOURS

The first step towards recovering from unhealthy behaviours is awareness, and admitting that we would benefit from letting go of old behaviours that won't serve us anymore.

Unhealthy and addictive behaviours in a romantic attachment can often be mistaken for feelings of deep love, but 'needing' the other person often stems from fear, lack of trust, neediness and dependency. Often this is only evident when we find ourselves in a state of crisis.

Unfortunately, few people are able to admit they need help to discover where their problems derive from. An unhealthy relationship can take many forms. Below are some of the symptoms you might be familiar with:

- You feel as if you can't live without the other person.
- You expect your partner to behave in a certain way.
- You blame others for how you feel.
- You feel better when you can control a situation and its outcome.
- You think it's acceptable to put yourself and your needs first/last.

IN THERAPY:

When I next saw the client, she complained that her husband never understood her when she talked about emotions or tried to share something emotionally. He was ok as long as she stayed with the facts, she said. It amazed her that she had been able to go on in this colourless life for so long.

In the beginning he was the one who always suggested journeys and holidays and arranged them and she felt looked after and introduced to adventures. She mistook that for his being in touch with his emotions. She said she came to this realisation after starting therapy. Her question now was: "Could he feel emotion or not?"

I presented his Family Map to her and showed her the line between his mother and father where her husband had written "absence of emotions". She replied: "I think I'd better go and live with an artist." She paused. "But I have the children. And the wonderful house that I've worked on. And the dog." Then she laughed. But she stopped laughing when she thought about how many of her friends had started commenting on the obvious issues she had with her husband and questioned why she wanted to stay in the marriage. "It's beginning to make me look like a failure and a loser," she said, expressing surprise that other people could see their problems with such clarity.

By looking at our Family Map and noticing the traits of the most important people in our lives and their behaviour, we start to identify our own patterns. We realise our positive and negative ways and can gradually start to open up and see our role in what is happening to us in our lives.

Eventually we are put in touch with our senses so we can achieve a state of awareness, where the real work of emotional recovery can take place. There can be a severe downside for those who are unable to share how they feel and choose instead to ignore their feelings. Sometimes in an effort to numb what people feel, they turn to substances, all kinds of addictions, even self-harm or seriously act out the pressure inside.

EXPLORING OUR EMOTIONAL RANGE

"It is by logic that we prove, but by intuition that we discover."

French mathematician Henri Poincaré (1854-1912)

It is interesting to note the author and psychotherapist Daniel H. Pink's view: "The future no longer belongs to people controlled by the left half of the brain, reasoning quickly and logically. For that we have computers. We are leaving the information society that has required rational and linear thinking, and moving into what I call the concept society. This means that those who create artistic and emotional values are better off, those who find patterns and see the bigger picture, who can tell stories and invent things people didn't know they wanted. All these competencies are controlled by the right part of the brain. Attributes associated with the left part of the brain are still necessary – but not enough!"

I FEEL, THEREFORE I AM

The French philosopher and mathematician René Descartes' (1596-1650) had a famous dualist theory: "I think and therefore I am."

The Dutch philosopher Spinoza (1632-1677) challenged this view in his masterwork *The Ethics,* arguing that the body and mind were not separate, but rather a connected whole. For centuries Spinoza's work was ignored, whereas Decartes rationalist doctrine immortalized him as a visionary and became the underlying principle of modern philosophy. The New York Times article (2003) *"I feel, Therefore I Am"* stated: "Science is proving Spinoza more current."

In the 1990s neuroscientist Dr. Antonio Damasio turned decades of scientific wisdom on its head with his breakthrough research. As he put it: "Neuroscience gave the cold shoulder to emotion." Feelings were considered "elusive, indescribable, too subjective." His books: *Descartes' Error: Emotion, Reason and the Human Brain* (1994) and *The Feeling of What Happens, Body and Emotion in the Making of Consciousness* (1999) were instrumental in the 'affect revolution,' and in 2003 *The Chronicle of Higher Education* reported that: "Academics are throwing themselves into the study of emotion with the rapturous intensity of a love affair."

If you are afraid of delving into the pain, it will stifle your growth. You might ask: "Is it safe to open up? Is it safe to get emotionally involved?" We can train to reprogram our own behaviour. But we cannot reprogram other people's behaviour.

The resistance to accessing our emotions can cause us to feel low, unhappy or depressed. Depression could be described as an umbrella term for trapped emotions. This can make us feel passive; we display resistance, procrastinate and become avoiders, among other symptoms. Eventually this leads us to various irrational behaviour like compulsion, obsession, unhealthy habits, dependence and addiction.

Emotions provide information that allows us to realise what is actually going on inside, and to some extent they lead to the path of recovery. By coming to accept our personal emotional lives we are affirming and valuing ourselves so we can become more skilful in handling all kind of emotions – including negative ones. Instead of fleeing from them and avoiding them, we stop fearing them and become integrated on all sides. In this guise, we can cope effectively and behave with more self-esteem.

At 12 Step meetings where people with addiction get together, they speak to the group, based on admitting their defects and sharing their experience strength and hope.

THE BRAIN MAP

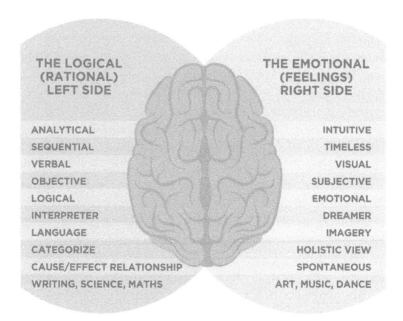

THE LOGICAL (RATIONAL) LEFT SIDE	THE EMOTIONAL (FEELINGS) RIGHT SIDE
ANALYTICAL	INTUITIVE
SEQUENTIAL	TIMELESS
VERBAL	VISUAL
OBJECTIVE	SUBJECTIVE
LOGICAL	EMOTIONAL
INTERPRETER	DREAMER
LANGUAGE	IMAGERY
CATEGORIZE	HOLISTIC VIEW
CAUSE/EFFECT RELATIONSHIP	SPONTANEOUS
WRITING, SCIENCE, MATHS	ART, MUSIC, DANCE

Giving people space is a particularly challenging issue in relationships and, therefore, it is essential to wait and to listen. Knowing 'when to speak' requires empathy and intuition. It's beneficial to learn how to find the fine balance between being a good listener and being a rational 'fixer'. If you can contain another person's pain you will be an invaluable asset.

IN THERAPY:

After several sessions with the couple independently of one another, I suggested all three of us should meet up. I presented my basic challenge: "Let's not end it, but instead let's mend it."

I asked if they were willing to make an effort to continue to work and explore how they could conduct their relationship in a better way.

I brought up the issue that conflict was an inevitable part of a relationship between spouses, parents and children and colleagues, as it was impossible not to have some disagreements. I highlighted the fact that it doesn't mean you've failed or let yourself down.

Because we have never been taught how to handle our emotions, we have never been taught how to handle a conflict situation either. We are scared of conflict. I asked how this had been dealt with in their respective families.

The wife described how her father had often been withdrawn and that once in a while he would get angry, especially when her mother would play the victim and cry.

The husband didn't offer to contribute to this subject, so I asked him what had happened in his home. "My main issue was my father's anger that could come out at me sometimes. My parents never seemed to be able to come to a solution because they could both be angry."

At this point, I realised he had changed his story. He was no longer describing his parents' relationship as "calm". I mentioned this to him and suggested that maybe he had built up this defence wall because of the impact of the pain and fear which would have been the consequence of his parents' conflicts.

I then discovered that his father and grandfather had been in the military so emotions could have been discouraged. It became clear that the message in his family has always been: "Just get on with it!"

I then introduced The Brain Map to show how the brain is metaphorically divided in two with the left side consisting of the rational components like analytical, logical and language; whilst the right side primarily presenting emotions, intuition and art.

The wife claimed the right side whilst he understood he belonged on the left side. With surprise, they realised why they had been finding it such a struggle to communicate with one another. In their case the two sides were not relating. They sat in silence. What were they going to do?

UNDERSTANDING OUR EMOTIONAL SYSTEM

Referring again to Susie Orbach, the well-known Founder of The Women's Institute, and psychotherapist, she says in her Radio BBC 3 lecture:

"Therapy is a challenge to the notion of the rational, or perhaps I should say, it limits what we understand as rational, and how far we can go with rationality as a concept. We live with the ideas of the subjective and the objective realms, often disparaging the former and elevating the latter as though they were in two entirely different modes of thinking, being and feeling. In truth, this division is unsustainable. Subjective and objective thoughts and feelings are the outcomes of different knowledge that are related. The subjective, which is often seen as personal, idiosyncratic and intuitive, sits on and is entwined with structures of thinking which are designated as logical, deductive and analytic. If we paused and consider how we use this vision, it becomes apparent that the way an individual (be they a barrister, a cook, a parent, or a dancer), makes a logical analytic argument, is always in reference to their own lived experience."

The Brain Map was a discovery for the couple. When I showed

them the map again, he read aloud the descriptions on each side and said: "Obviously I belong on the left side." I asked him where he thought his wife belonged. He didn't hesitate: "Oh, the right side!" Then he asked: "Does this mean I don't share my emotions?" She immediately responded: "This is a moment I've looked forward to for years!" He replied: "Well I don't think this has anything to do with why we don't get on!" He looked confused.

I explained to him the importance of a more open communication with her stating that otherwise unmet needs could lead to resentment and hurt feelings. He explained his life was about being the man, going out and earning the money, protecting his family and fighting his way to the top. He concluded: "Like most men, I have no time for feelings!"

Over the last decades researching the brain, and due to advanced scanner systems like the PET Scan, we have learnt that the brain contains billions of neural pathways. They land in our metaphorical "software" and the consequences are that we seem to have stored most of what we have ever experienced. This gives support to the notion that in the main part we react to a feeling that we have already experienced.

In his book, *In The Brain: A Secret History* (BBC 2011) Dr. Michael Mosley investigated the deeply irrational and complex part of our mind: emotions. One of the founding fathers of American behavioural psychology, psychologist John B. Watson (1878-1958) asked three simple questions: "Where do emotions come from? Are we born with them? Do we learn them?" He thought that we are all born with three basic emotions: love, fear and anger, and that the mix of these created the emotional range we experience as adults. He believed that the emotions we experienced or felt later in life were a product of our childhood experiences, determining whom we would fall in love with, our fears and the triggers that would make us angry.

IN THERAPY:

In the following session with the wife on her own we studied the Family Map again and focused on her husband's father and his Grandfather. These were the two men closest to him, who were as already discovered from an authoritarian military background and as a consequence, it would seem her husband was not used to emotional feedback or validation of his feelings.

The wife told me: "It often made me so angry thinking about what we could have had, but most of all angry for his choice that he would rather be right than have a relationship with me. He would give it up for the sake of staying behind that wall you told me about."

"How about his anger?"

She said he had a tendency to criticise and use dominance and control rather than give in to overt anger.

I pointed out that the person behind The Wall (in this case her husband,) had no idea that he was behind a wall as his current mental position came from the subconscious mechanism from early childhood. It's like the brain has given a message "Don't think about what you feel. Survive."

"So how could he do this to me?" she asked. I explained that the whole point of someone being behind The Wall is that they are operating from a predetermined system or instinct, like a pattern. I told her that she wouldn't be asking that question if he were a manic-depressive or an addict, or an alcoholic. This is where acceptance comes in.

WE ARE NOT OUR BEHAVIOUR

From the earliest point in our lives we have heard the phrase:

"You have to change! If you don't change you won't get the best out of yourself." What is vital for succeeding in implementing any possible changes in ourselves and others, is the realisation that we are not our behaviour. Our behaviour is separate from us. This realisation can free us, and makes it easier for us to overcome resistance to change.

One way of looking at change in the context of behaviour is to consider how behaviours would benefit if the person changed. This is where it's good to look at the Family Map and understand your partner, their family members, their colleagues and others.

Referring again to Robert Burney, he describes how we learn and develop our behaviour in his book *Codependence: The Dance of Wounded Souls*:

> "We learned to have a dysfunctional relationship with self, with other people, and with life in early childhood. It is vital to start looking at ourselves and life from a whole new perspective, with different eyes. In order to do that, it is necessary to start being honest with our self. The first step is to admit to ourselves that we need help in order to see our reality with more clarity, so that we can start changing our relationships and the way we define our needs in life. Only then can we unlearn old behaviour and start to discover new ways towards developing healthy relationships with self and others."

WHAT ROLE DID I PLAY?

Whenever a difficult situation happens or reoccurs, it's time for self-reflection and to ask yourself: "What was my role in this? What behaviour did I engage in? Did I do anything to provoke this?" We need to consider how we tackle the power dilemma where we might be patronised by our partner or through lack of understanding or ignorance.

IN THERAPY:

In the wife's next session she said to me: "Why are you asking me what role I played in the conflict?" She expressed anger and irritation about her husband's inability to share anything emotional, and then examined the information about his background and understood he couldn't do emotions. She had fought for this for years only to find that he had been preconditioned by the circumstances of his childhood to resist emotions. The only solution now would be for her to assume a new attitude herself.

In an article in *Psychology Today*, the well know American psychotherapist, Andrea Brandt says: "People carry childhood emotional wounds into adulthood. One way these wounds reveal themselves is through the creation of a false self. Children make meaning out of events they witness and the things that happen to them and create an internal map of how their world is. But if children don't create a new internal map as they grow up, their old way of interpreting the world can damage their ability to function as adults."

UNPLEASANT BEHAVIOURS THAT SUPPORT THE WALL

* Manipulations/Charm
* Dominance/Control/Defensiveness

- Criticism/Belittling/Contempt
- Anger – Passive or Aggressive
- Competition/Winning/Superiority
- Blame/Scapegoating/Shame
- Emotional blackmail/Disdain/Mocking/ Divisiveness
- Violence/Physical abuse
- Rationalisation/Justification
- Bamboozling/Confusion (lying, forgetting, gas-lighting, crazy-making)

CHAPTER 5

Why We Build Walls

WE ALL NEED TO be seen, heard, understood and confirmed but often we haven't developed access to what makes this possible.

The difficulty in accessing our emotions is a result of the way that we have been conditioned through centuries. We have been taught to cultivate the rational.

The table on the following page illustrates the imbalance between the left and right brain values in our education system, at work, in society and even in our relationships. We don't get rewards for developing our emotions intuitions, empathy, dreamer, the arts, dance.

The highlighted qualities on the right side indicate a person who has no ability to connect with intuition, emotions, day dreams or have a holistic view.

Left Hemisphere	Right Hemisphere
Analytical	Intuitive
Sequential	Timeless
Verbal	Visual
Objective	Subjective
Logical	Emotions
Interpreter	Dreamer
Language	Imagery
Categorize	Holistic view
Cause/effect relationship	Spontaneous
Writing, science, maths	Art, music, dance

DISCOVERING NEGATIVE DEFENCE MECHANISMS

The result of living with somebody behind The Wall, or by being behind The Wall ourselves, is that we are prevented from accessing something we all seek subconsciously which is emotional intimacy, being connected with, belonging to, being part of, and being at one with someone. The irony is that it is only we who prevent ourselves from obtaining this.

The Wall is like a defensive cover for who we really are and reduces quality of life for both the person behind it and the one in front of it.

It is a form of protection against the pain and shame in admitting we have feelings we don't understand and don't know how to deal with. One feeling that makes us feel afraid is shame. Shame can make us feel bad, and when we feel bad we might even come to believe we are bad. When children don't have their needs met they feel a sense of shame, as if they weren't good enough. When we are young we need to feel valued and appreciated and can't manufacture those feelings on our own.

Little by little our subconscious mind starts to build a barrier of protection that we hide behind to feel safe and to protect our vulnerability. This is The Wall. Fear plays a significant part in its construction. Based on the flee and flight mentality, the person not getting validation and getting hurt needs to protect themselves, and the best way to do this is to hide. The Wall becomes their fort.

DYSFUNCTIONAL BEHAVIOURS

The Recipient also has defence mechanisms, different from the ones we have described so far, and is subconsciously attracted to people with the same conditions and unhealed wounds.

We then end up repeating our past patterns of hurt, fear, anger, abuse, betrayal, shame, guilt and abandonment. We let them into our lives because they bring out feelings that seem familiar to us, that we adopted in early life.

The Wall Hider knows exactly which emotional buttons to press in the Recipient and the Recipient falls. In time the Recipient comes to live in hope. In the hope that, with love and commitment, The Wall Hider will change and everything will get better.

The dramas we create in our own lives are often old patterns, ingrained and embedded in one of our multitude neural pathways. We tend to replay our family dynamics, but in a new setting or relationship. The challenge is to understand that we are playing out the same old stories from our family pattern again and again. Once we realise this, which normally comes through therapeutic channels, we can move to implement a new signalling system. In doing this we develop a greater awareness of self and of others and, going forward, attract people who are less damaged.

IN THERAPY:

In the following session the couple seemed more open. We agreed that each of them should come with a Family Map. When the wife was given her husband's map she expressed surprise at the extent of the existing character traits that made him who he was. When the husband studied his wife's map he asked: "What do you mean by saying you are there for others?" She smiled and said: "Haven't you noticed that in all these years?" He answered he could see the same qualities in her mother. The wife acknowledged that looking at her personality in the context of the Family Map allowed her to see herself and understand that self in a different way. "I admit I hadn't been aware of that before," she told me. She then waited to see whether her husband would admit to seeing facets of his personality that he hadn't recognised before, but he didn't say anything.

CHAPTER 6

Connecting the Bricks

THE BUILDING OF THE Wall derives from Pride.

The bricks that follow come from a fear of being seen as weak, not good enough or stupid. The subsequent bricks come from the fear of admitting that we have specific flaws and from this comes denial. The way of dealing with denial is self-righteousness or the need to be right which cultivates self-justification. At this point we are unable to imagine behaving in any other way.

IN THERAPY:

I explained to the husband that we had to work on finding a way to make some changes in his behaviour and I emphasised the rewards that this would bring. I anticipated that he would resist change and therefore focused on staying positive when looking at the outcome.

The reward would be that his wife would be happier and would stay with him. Further, these changes would help with some of the work issues and benefit his relationship with his children. He responded by asking what this change would entail. I answered by showing him the image of The Wall, and asked which of the behaviours related to him. He said he needed time to absorb the new idea.

When I next saw his wife, we discussed his reaction. I shared with her that he had arrived at a point where he understood some changes to his behaviour were essential if they were to continue with their relationship. I indicated that he might need guidance from her, not in the shape of blame but in terms of setting boundaries. We agreed that he may not like our plan, but I reassured her in my opinion he wanted to keep her and would therefore be more open to guidance and change than he was before. In my experience with other clients The Wall Hider (if still around at this point), is invariably unwilling to compromise. But suddenly the wife had a complete change of heart. "I'm not sure I'm good enough," she said.

THE COST OF PRIDE

There is a commonality in The Walls we build, with a few variations. Because we are not all alike, The Wall will vary and consist of different 'bricks' as the paragraphs below illustrate.

Pride is the main disguise for the following 'defence mechanisms': fear of being seen as weak, fear of admitting, denial, self-righteousness and self-justification. Our first instinct is to hide unpleasant feelings to cover emotions we even cannot

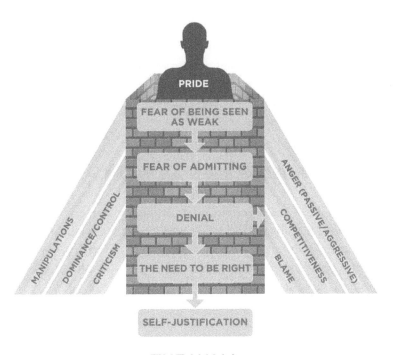

THE WALL

The Bricks in The Wall Consist of:	Behaviours to Support The Wall:
Pride	Manipulation
Fear of being seen as weak	Dominance/control
Fear of admitting	Criticism
Denial	Anger (passive and aggressive)
The need to be right	Competitiveness
Self-justification	Blame

admit we have. We start by building pride.

Pride is a precursor to a fear of admitting that we have emotions and feelings like shame, guilt, fear, grief, sadness, disappointment and so on. It stems from growing up in dysfunctional families or being in unhealthy relationships that did not meet our emotional needs and expectations.

FEAR OF BEING SEEN AS WEAK

The fear of being seen as weak, stupid or not good enough, powerless, humiliated and guilty are so powerful that instead of admitting we have these feelings, we start to construct a fortress and hence the beginning of The Wall starts to take shape to protect the vulnerability.

Fear of rejection, guilt, failure, stupidity, not being good enough, making a mistake, being at fault, having a blunder that feels like a failure or a defeat all result in us feeling vulnerable, weak and exposed. This is actually the opposite of what we want to obtain subconsciously, which is to connect with others, to be accepted and to be loved.

With the evolution of our emotions combined with the various traumas of our childhood, we move to defending ourselves, therein building a defence mechanism automatically. This process becomes so vital to our being that we are unable to see any other way of behaving and start operating in a constant state of defence. Therefore, the idea of admitting we are wrong is distorted and confused. If we admit we're wrong, we're seen as weak. In fact, it should be seen as a virtue instead of a failure.

FEAR OF ADMITTING

Counsellor Aine Haeger says: "It just doesn't feel good and it hurts our pride. We live in a competitive society where mistakes are often frowned upon. When we admit fault, it can feel like we lost or we're just not good enough. It shows a side of ourselves that we sometimes want to keep hidden from other people because it shows that we are not perfect and have faults."

Clinical psychologist Jan Harrell believes it's a basic animal survival instinct. We instinctively respond as though we fear we will be killed if we are vulnerable. Because we are a society that focuses on right and wrong, checks and balances, people do not like to admit fault or show fear as they think this diminishes them in the eyes of others, which leads to their own sense of self-worth suffering.

DENIAL

Denial sits right in the centre of The Wall. It's an obvious negative state that blocks what we are looking for in our interaction with others: the connection or the flow between people.

It is a behavioural display of self-deception and false beliefs found in many of us. The opening page in the book *Denial* by Ajit Varki describes denial as follows: "An unconscious defence mechanism characterised by the refusal to acknowledge painful realities, thoughts or feelings."

It is a sub-conscious defence mechanism and, therefore, the person who is in such a state is incapable of admitting it. It's a natural element of their being and they are not aware of any wrongdoing when in denial. They refuse to accept reality, and denial becomes the solution against their feelings of anxiety, guilt, shame or not being good enough. This state is, in many ways, the opposite of taking responsibility for our emotions and all that is going on around us.

Denial minimises our fear and can be one way of denying reality or avoiding seeing things as they really are. Justifying aggression and not taking responsibility, direct attention away from us by denying the impact our behaviour has on another person. The consequences are that we avoid guilt and this in turn prevents us from showing remorse for or empathy towards the other person. This can obviously be extremely painful for the other.

JAMIE'S STORY:

Jamie, 38, a painter came to see me saying he was in a desperate situation. He was having a close relationship with Elle, a gallery owner in her late fifties, who he assumed could help him on his way to becoming a recognized artist. He had shown promise when he left art school at 25, but had spent years trying to establish himself.

He told me Elle was well placed in the art world and sometimes took him to private viewings. She was in a position to introduce him to influential personalities. They often got on well, laughed at the same things and enjoyed the viewings and their creative discussions. And as member of the prestigious boards like the V&A, Elle could promote his career if she chose to. He emphasized this.

She seemed possessive of her children, they still lived with her although they were both in their twenties. He understood the daughter Kate, 22, had difficulties holding on to a job and felt stuck in finding an emotional direction in her life. He told me how Elle had asked him for help as she knew he had gone through a similar dilemma in his early life.

He talked to Kate, who told him about a man that she couldn't resist who often took advantage of her. She told him that after their interactions she would feel remorse and shame. Jamie felt he had been a positive influence in trying to help Kate

But now he was sitting in front of me, very upset and on the verge of crying. With his head in his hands he exclaimed: "I just can't believe it. She was furious with me!" Jamie relayed to me how Elle had screamed at him saying:

"I should never have let you near her." He said his heart had stopped at her outburst and he was struggling to understand what he had done wrong.

When he had asked Elle she had replied: "How dare you ask my daughter why she always sleeps with married men and breaks up marriages? She says she forbids me to see you ever again and that I have to get you out my life. You have upset her so much and I am very concerned. How dare you tell her she's a marriage wrecker and only goes with married men because she can't get a man of her own. You've said other things I can't even bring myself to repeat."

Jamie sank further in his chair and seemed inconsolable. We sat in silence for quite a while, then he said: "It feels like she's betrayed me. She asked me to help, which I did – the best I could – and then she turns it against me with a dagger!" Jaime said he had tried to make things right by explaining to Elle why he had said the things he had. At the same time, he suggested that Kate might have manipulated the conversation somewhat because she wanted attention. Elle had been furious at this and told him never to accuse her daughter of lying. Jaime tried to speak to Kate but she refused to see him. In the end he got angry and got into a conflict with Elle.

"How dare you ask me to try and help Kate first and then when I do, turn on me. I feel betrayed." Elle told him coldly that she had only passed on information from Kate that she thought he would find helpful and had not expected him to send her 31 texts ending their friendship.

Jamie asked me how Elle could misrepresent all she had said and accused him of. He asked whether she was changing her tune because she didn't want to lose him. I told him this: "Here Elle is a clear example of somebody who cannot admit any wrongdoing and justifies her behaviour by twisting the truth. This person is someone hiding behind a wall. Maybe it's now easier to understand that she is not likely to admit her mistake or accept any wrongdoing."

I explained more about what a Wall Hider was and he agreed that he had seen many signs of it before which had confused him. In the end his need of her was too practical. It was about survival. After a few disagreeable days he went back to her, but with the knowledge that their relationship would never be the same.

For me Elle was a prime example of somebody who could never admit being wrong and was always right. She was hiding behind The Wall.

THE NEED TO BE RIGHT

In his book *The Addictive Personality*, author Craig Nakken writes:

> "For the power-centred person everything flows from the premise of being right which gives the illusion of control and bolsters self-confidence but not self-esteem. Being wrong is a sign of failure and weakness and throws the individual into vulnerable fearful place. Being right invests power and righteousness in the individual."

This describes what happens to a person who lives in the pursuit of being right all the time and seems to be the foundation of The Wall. It serves to justify everything. In this situation, the other behaviours in The Wall can't be questioned because they are right! The result is that the connection or flow between two people in a couple is adversely impacted.

SELF-JUSTIFICATION

Self-justification or self-justified behaviour is frequent in the way we interact. It is evident regardless of whether we are right or wrong, and can be seen in the way in which we communicate. Justified emotions and actions go hand-in-hand. This means that the person behind The Wall who is using their defence mechanisms, will feel justified irrespective of what their behaviours might be. This makes it even harder, as when trying to raise the issue of behaviour with someone behind The Wall, it won't even occur to him or her that they could or should behave differently.

THE STRUCTURE OF THE WALL

We implement strategies to support the wall and keep it standing. Among these you will find: manipulation, dominance, control, criticism, anger, blame.

These behaviours increase its resistance. What happens as a consequence is that emotions build up over time and turn into resentment.

It's essential to understand that we are able to change these defence mechanisms and replace them with healthier bricks, but first we have to understand the bricks from which our wall is built, and the behaviours we need to change in order for it to fall.

I'm inspired by Leonard Cohen when he says: "There is a crack in everything, that's how the light gets in." With this in mind we can start to work with the bricks we have with better and healthier defence mechanisms. But first let's have a closer look at the unhealthy behaviours that keep it standing in the first place.

IN THERAPY:

When I next saw the couple the session was taken up by his inability to see himself and the role he played in his wife's frustration. He refused to see that he was the cause of many of the disputes He simply couldn't be wrong. On one rare occasion he admitted he could be wrong, but when invited to explain what he thought had caused the conflict, he said it was his wife's constant criticism of him. His wife declared this to be unfair and started crying. She said she was now at a point she had hoped never to reach. The husband asked what she meant. She told him that she didn't feel nurtured or loved and that he couldn't bring out the real female she was. She said that she had tried her best but that now she'd had enough. She got up slowly and walked out.

He stood up but was clearly feeling a bit thrown by his wife's comment. Then he laughed. He said to me: "I don't think a bunch of flowers is going to do it this time." He waited for my reaction. "Do you?" he asked. We sat in silence then heard the door leading to the street close behind his wife. The silence continued. We knew she wasn't coming back.

Suddenly he said: "If she does this to me she will regret it. I won't put up with this." I asked what he wanted to do. He said: "This is my employer's fault. He's loaded too much on me for too long. This I will not accept." I replied: "We have to take her reaction seriously." He moved to leave then turned and asked me: "What can I do?"

I invited him to sit down and asked him: "What role did you play in this?" He paused. "Maybe I did not show that I appreciated her." The bricks started to crumble. He covered his face with his hands. "Is this it?" he questioned. He looked up and I was almost surprised by how frightened he seemed.

CHAPTER 7

Negative Behaviours That Support the Wall

MANIPULATION

IT IS NOT EASY to detect manipulation, as it comes from subtle games the other person plays. When we come from families where manipulation hasn't been a feature it's even more difficult to detect. Manipulation is based on another person needing something from you. This can be anything from money, being "taken care of", a place to live, help with a project etc. The need to feel in control by creating uncertainty and doubt by making another feel valued and loved one moment, and uncertain and inadequate the next. A Manipulator can switch from showing no respect or care, to making you feel good about yourself, then bringing you down again by criticism.

So how can a Manipulator make another feel valued and strong for his or her own motive? There are a number of ways to do this: by giving positive feedback, abstaining from criticism and blame, being attentive to the other's needs, making future plans together and giving the recipient more attention so he/she is seen, heard, understood and acknowledged.

That feel-good factor is such a powerful sensation it'll come to be a happy drug that the recipient might feel addicted to. However, this state of contentment can change, either suddenly or subtly, and the effects of this can be disturbing. If the attention the recipient enjoyed is being withheld or withdrawn, the recipient can start to panic and fear they are losing their partner. This is exactly what the Manipulator wants as this gives him or her the feeling of having power over the other.

The truth is that the Manipulator himself or herself might have low self esteem so putting somebody down can alleviate that feeling As already said a Manipulator often wants something from the other. The Manipulator functions from a basis of deception. He or she has used his/her charm over a period of time to ensnare and beguile others into a relationship. Once the Manipulator is confident that the other is comfortably established, they can start their games. They turn around things the recipient said to confuse, or deny even though the recipient knows differently.

Another behaviour often used to confuse the partner is when the Manipulator can suddenly become a victim. This often happens if the Manipulator feels criticised or blamed. "How can you do this to me?" This might make the partner feel guilty and even apologise. The Manipulator will then use this and might say something like: "There you see – you're in the wrong!"

SHAME

Shame is the feeling we dread the most. It's a place where we are not valued or not worthy of respect, where we feel ashamed of who we are. Being able to cause a feeling of shame in a partner is attractive to the Manipulator. He/she might threaten to leave the relationship which ties into the greatest fear of his/her partner. This is the point at which the Manipulator feels most powerful and feels able to obtain what he/she wants. A Manipulator will use control, dominance, criticism, passive or aggressive anger, competitiveness and blame. Shame can keep us isolated and distanced from others therefore sabotaging our desire for intimacy.

IN THERAPY:

Interestingly, after what happened in the previous session, it was now the husband who was eager to come and see me sooner rather than later. He insisted that his wife should be there. After some discussion, she agreed to arrive on her own and meet him in the session. They had not spoken since the last one.

The husband's behaviour couldn't have been more different this time. He was attentive to his wife from the moment she came in and smiled to welcome her. I wondered if this was his way of controlling her. I invited him to talk first and he was quick to start. "I don't think I understood until now. I simply want you in my life, on my side. I have heard so many times in this room that I can't admit things, and maybe for the first time, I admit I've never understood the meaning or importance of that. But a few days ago at work an incident happened that made me see things differently."

He went on to describe how his boss had made a mistake

and instead of admitting it had been his fault and apologising, he had blamed someone else. "All of us around him knew it had been his fault and not anyone else's but we all stayed quiet," he added. "So on the way home I remembered you, both at home and here, when you have complained that I always had to be right."

His wife looked surprised and said: "I'm so glad you could see this in your boss. He's probably been doing this for years without you really noticing how painful it can be. As a result you behaved the same way with me."

The incident with his boss served to act as a point of reference between them. Sharing what they felt, allowed them to help each other and recognise that they had been stuck when it came to the way they each communicated

The wife used the opportunity to express that she needed his support with the children and noted how she sometimes reacted when he sided with their son. He said he understood but felt his son needed more support sometimes. At this point I made the suggestion that they should agree when in front of their son and discuss their respective feelings or issues when alone together.

The session ended with the couple agreeing to continue with therapy for the time being and then left together. I wondered whether he had controlled the situation, and if he would be able to let some of the aspects that had contributed to his Wall to dissipate and allow him to rebuild a new, better relationship.

We left it a few weeks before meeting again as it had been the start of the summer holidays and I wanted to give the couple time to explore the different atmosphere between them. In those weeks, the wife had been abroad visiting her parents with the children. The husband had been at home doing work on the house. He shared how that had given him the opportunity to reflect on what life would be like if he were living on his own. He described that feeling as being unsettling. The fact that he was about to share his vulnerability and talk about his fear made it clear that he had made a choice.

The wife said she felt that something radical had changed in him during the summer. She said, "We can even sit together and talk about the children, and how to encourage them to do small tasks at home. We can still disagree about things, but we are able to listen to each other, and I am much less irritated and angry with him. For years I felt I couldn't reach him but now he is more open, which gives me the courage to ask what I need from him in the way we communicate."

We decided to have a break after one more individual session with each of them.

DOMINANCE AND CONTROL

In a good relationship there is no need to control the other person, there is trust. It is a lack of trust that creates the need for control. This issue is common in all kind of relationships. It might be that our need to control stems from a deeply embedded fear of losing, which often relates back to a childhood trauma. When you are with a person who operates behind The Wall, control is an inevitable part of the relationship regardless of the fact that the other person won't like it or might not be willing to accept it. This is because, to the person behind The Wall, being controlling is entirely justifiable.

And as we know only too well, when we are in a relationship with somebody with a thick defence and give them even the slightest feedback, they quickly spit back with blame: "It's your fault!"

CRITICISM

Criticism is the killer in a relationship. When I watch a couple shoot each other down with criticism, I stop them after a while and ask: "Do you really think that he or she will change if you keep on like that?"

Both parties will invariably look at me in surprise, and one of them is likely to say: "But I'm just trying to make him see what he's doing wrong. He's so stubborn!"

How people go about criticising one another can vary. It is a marker used by our parents for evaluating or correcting our behaviour. It naturally occurs throughout our life in many different forms. In relationships, it can be deadly.. But it's only when we come to see that this behaviour doesn't serve us anymore, that we can start to act differently to form healthier relationships with ourselves and others.

ANGER – PASSIVE/AGGRESSIVE

Anger is one of our core feelings and our most primal one. It's a reaction to emotions deeply ingrained to defend the tribe we grew up in, our country, our territory, our village, our community. It's the opposite of flight – it's fight!

Anger can often be found on The Family Map as it's related to our genes. It's a behaviour that has been repeated throughout generations and passed on, playing out again and again in our childhood. It's therefore one of the feelings that we believe to be justifiable.

It can be extremely unpleasant and frightening for somebody who hasn't experienced anger in their family dynamic, and can be detrimental to family life and any kind of relationship. Anger plays a big part in the emotional make-up of people who live behind The Wall and can be played out in two ways. The traditional way in which we perceive anger to be demonstrated is through aggression or violence. But it can also be played out as passive anger.

Passive-aggressive behaviour is an insidious way to manipulate another person. The behaviour will often belong to a person who is subconsciously afraid of her/his own angry feelings, so find a way to withhold their anger instead. Passive aggressive behaviour can be so subtle that it can take a long time for a person in the relationship who is at the receiving end to understand and even accept what is going on.

The person with passive aggressive tendencies uses this behaviour to empower themselves. It can take many forms. Somebody practising this behaviour can, confuse and stir up anger until the other explodes and acts out the tension between them. The passive/aggressive will then blame that person saying: "Its obvious you are the angry one."

The passive/aggressive might even walk out of a room while their partner is talking. They might not follow up on something that has been promised or deny that a certain event was ever planned. They may refuse to answer any questions.

COMPETITIVENESS

Competitiveness is meant to be a healthy drive to achieve goals. But competition between people can be negative and even destructive. Most inventions probably derive from a drive of wanting to be better than another, or from a place of wanting to show someone you can do something special. Competition can add great value to a relationship, particularly after the initial stage of pure admiration has passed.

In the wrong environment, competition can be one of the

ways of demeaning the other party. It can lead to the other person feeling that there is something wrong with them, that they are not good enough or not worthy enough. Where you are dealing with a partner who lives behind The Wall, this is exactly how they want to make you feel because that bolsters their ego. They feel this behaviour is acceptable.

BLAME

When we feel attacked or judged we either blame others or we blame ourselves. That attack could be direct verbal blame, a look, a tone of voice, or someone saying something we interpreted in the wrong way.

If we are attacked and the attacker is justified, we might feel like a loser and interpret the comments of our attacker as a critical parental voice. If we do not consider the attack to be right we might attack back to prove the attacker wrong, thereby passing blame.

Blame can derive from different sources. For many it can be a completely natural and instant reaction to whatever comes their way. It is often used to alleviate pain, or in a situation where a person is not capable of taking responsibility for their own emotions. Blame is detrimental to any relationship and is often a pattern that starts in an early phase of our life, as a default setting in the family's dynamic. Defending ourselves by using blame seems to be part of the evolution of human beings. So how do we deal with it? We recognise the difference between feedback and criticism and share it.

REACHING THE PERSON BEHIND THE WALL

Many of my clients react in the same way when they are presented with an image of The Wall. They come to the awakening that whilst they may be able to better recognise their partners by understanding The Wall, they may never be able to reach them, and further that the possibility of achieving change is limited or unlikely. They see that their options are to either understand their partner and accept or tolerate his/her behaviour whilst trying to manifest some level of change. Or to leave.

CHAPTER 8

The Power of Acceptance

"Acceptance is hard to comprehend. I thought if I accepted something, that means I liked it and I wanted it to stay. But this is not what acceptance is. Acceptance means being honest about what is happening in my life, what I am thinking, and what I am feeling. When I can stop denying and rebelling against myself, I can relax and let go of the control. When I stop trying to control, I am open to the learning and healing which are waiting for me."

Today, Emotions Anonymous.

IN THERAPY:

When I saw the wife on her own she said she felt more grounded and was less nervous of him. I suggested that she might now like to start sharing more of herself with him in a confident manner. I told her to expect that he would probably blame her again, and that when he does she should make it clear she will no longer accept it. I counselled her to gently ask him if this attack of blame was really what he wanted to be doing, so that he would become more aware of the behaviour patterns ingrained in him.

When the husband came for his session we focused on the notion of change. I asked him how he felt at the thought of implementing different behaviour patterns. I showed him the design of The Wall and highlighted those behaviours acted out to support The Wall. I explained that the behaviour of blame is often the most difficult for the person who does it to admit or even understand.

I explained that it would be beneficial if he could recognise the part he played when he and his wife found themselves in conflict. I asked him to think about how his behaviours could change the result of a conflict situation in the future. He looked thoughtful. I continued by suggesting that his wife could help by sharing more of what upset her and further ways for the relationship to work. I even suggested she set some boundaries. He nodded and said (somewhat to my surprise): "Yes, I will need help to behave in another way. I will try!" I told him that we were here to support him and we agreed to continue the sessions on a monthly basis to keep the momentum and good will going.

Both the husband and wife left the session pleased about what they had achieved. They set the intention of spending more time together and said they understood that a good relationship needed to be nurtured.

BEHAVIOURAL SCAFFOLDING

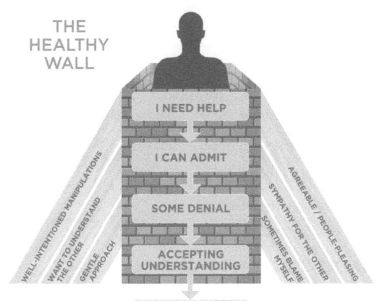

The Wall Hider suffers from:	Behaviours of The Wall Hider
Low self-worth	Manipulation
Needing help	Want to understand the other
Varying levels of admittance	Submissive
Varying levels of denial	Agreeable/people pleaser
Lack of empathy	Sympathy for the other
Self-doubt	Blame myself

A Short Course In Human Relations:	
The 6 most important words	I admit that I was wrong
The 5 most important words	You did a great job
The 4 most important words	What do you think?
The 3 most important words	Could you please
The 2 most important words	Thank you
The most important word	We
The least important word	I

UNDERSTANDING OUR BEHAVIOUR

THE HEALTHY WALL

Healthy Traits:	Healthy Wall Behaviours:
Confidence	Healthy Manipulations
Self-Reliance	Open-mindedness
Being able to admit	Acceptance
Not being in denial	Able to see the other's point of view
Open to self-insight	Doesn't need to be right
Good Self-Esteem	Doesn't blame others

The most important point to be aware of, is that it's highly improbable that anyone behind The Wall will change without a considerable amount of work. It may be painful to admit this, but when we start to see and feel the truth, it can feel liberating. We can then begin to profit from understanding what is actually happening which leads to acceptance. It is at this point that you can start to evaluate whether you wish to stay or to leave?

JOHN'S STORY:

The relationship started well. I met a woman a while ago, and after getting to know her, moved into her house. This seemed to suit her because I could contribute to the household costs. We had seemed compatible and I was definitely attracted to her until she began asking probing questions every time I went out.

She would ask a series of questions, then once I had answered them all things would go back to normal. After a few weeks the behaviour would start again. The questions were things like: "Why did I have to go out with my friends? What time was I going to be back? Why couldn't she come when I was out with the boys?" I started to feel that something wasn't quite right but couldn't put my finger on it. I started to doubt myself. Was I doing something wrong? Was I not good enough? I realised that I still liked her and wanted it to go back to how it was.

Then one day I saw her lose her temper with her own children. She exhibited extreme rage. Once she had finished scolding her children, she started on me. When I spoke to my male friends about what was going on they suggested I leave, or talk to a counsellor. I discounted it because I didn't think anyone would understand what I was going through. I was also somewhat trapped financially because I had given up my flat, and didn't have enough in savings for a deposit on another place. I couldn't see any light.

One day I was in a work meeting and ended up sitting next to a woman I found it very easy to talk to. It turned out she was a therapist. I made an appointment to go and talk to her in an official capacity. She told me the way for me to understand the situation better was to look at my childhood. She had me fill out a sheet called The Family Map.

The Family Map highlighted a pattern I had with my mother, who had a tendency to criticise me and belittle me. As a consequence, part of me still believed I deserved to be treated like that.

In my relationship, I found that I couldn't talk or discuss anything as my partner always had to be right and could never admit to be at fault or to having done something wrong. Everything was always my fault.

When I was shown an image of The Wall, all that I had struggled to understand became clear. I hadn't previously realised the importance of seeing a visual image, but the picture of The Wall resonated with me. I could see how the bricks helped to conceal the true identity of the person behind The Wall and allowed them to hide. I could also recognise from the support beams of The Wall, some of the behaviours that my partner used to keep The Wall up.

This was a breakthrough! Everything that was shown fitted my partner to the letter. It was an immense relief to be understood and to be able to see the emotional pattern of my partner. The fact that the behaviours formed a pattern made it clear to me that if she remained behind The Wall she would likely never change.

A few weeks after my discovery of The Wall, I managed to escape the house. I moved to a hostel and started to build my life for "me". Being free felt amazing. Now I look forward to every day. I set myself a goal to help others and was able to help the homeless, which gives me a great sense of fulfilment and a lot of energy, but that's another story!

BOUNDARIES

Boundaries allow us to build our self-esteem and thereby feel safe and empowered simply because we communicate our self-worth and who we are to our surroundings. When we maintain these boundaries we attract deeper self-love, respect and support in our relationships, as well as the communities we engage with. Our boundaries can protect us from engaging in unhealthy behaviours and enable us to say no to unreasonable demands from others.

EMMA'S STORY:

The problem for me started when my husband's career went badly. His failure at work became increasingly apparent and as it did so, he took less pride in my work and in my successes.

Often, I would hear little more than criticism. He would throw demeaning jabs at me or try to control me or the children. He frequently blamed being in a bad mood on me, as if there was something wrong with me and I was overbearing, high-maintenance, and demanding. I was multitasking and stressed with being a mother, wife and the main breadwinner in the family.

Women have fought to have it all for centuries, but it turned out that for me 'all' was way too much. I needed more support, not just financially but emotionally. The intimacy between us gradually started to dwindle. My husband was brilliant with the children and in the kitchen, but this meant that I began to feel pushed aside from the feminine roles which had previously given me pleasure. Instead I was permanently attached to my computer and near-addicted to my work. Meanwhile my husband seemed unable to thank me for my efforts and became more and more distanced as he battled with his lack of productivity.

I could literally feel his resentment of me growing and see a cold front building. He stopped wanting to spend time with me. We stopped having fun. We started to argue about money. And, whilst my world was getting bigger and I was meeting new people and travelling for work, his was shrinking. He was ready to settle for less, where I was ready to fly. When I tried talking to him about it, he couldn't verbalize his discontent or admit it.

A colleague recommended that I talk to someone, and when I finally met with a psychotherapist, I felt a huge relief. When she showed me an image of The Wall everything started to make sense. The psychotherapist explained the idea of visualising what we are going through when we live with someone behind The Wall. I could see that his pride was a method of protection and that he couldn't admit any failings for being seen as weak, not good or not clever enough.

The fear of admitting meant that my script and his were very different. His self-righteousness had felt like bullying at times and I could now see that his subtle controls were in fact acts of passive anger, ending in blame. I would go so far as to say that I actually grew fearful of him, even though I knew he would not harm me physically.

Now, I am learning to see patterns. I have found it empowering to understand what the game is, and can see how The Wall rose between us like a wedge in our marriage. I am at a point where I need to decide if I can accept these behaviours and live with them. Or if I can work on my own boundaries to save energy and self-esteem. My therapist has been a huge help and support and I continue to stay close to her and turn to her at challenging times.

According to the book *Denial – Self-Deception and False Beliefs* by Ajit Varki, denial is: "An unconscious defence mechanism characterised by refusal to acknowledge painful realities, thoughts or feelings. It results when one is unable to move away from the importance of being right, which partners are often both addicted to."

SELF-ACCEPTANCE

In his book, Varki looks at self-acceptance, saying: "Many have done a lot of harm to themselves, but when they start self-acceptance they can begin making amends." He says that one of the best ways to do this is to continually speak and think well of ourselves. In doing this, we reprogram our inner self-talk to a positive wavelength which feeds into self-acceptance.

Often we might repeat negative self-beliefs or self-disgust which produce a behaviour counter-productive to self-acceptance. People have a tendency to put themselves down by constantly saying or thinking they are not good enough, or that they can't do something, or that they are weak or that nobody cares about them. "I will never amount to anything," "I am fat," "I am disgusting." The list of negative comments we feed ourselves is endless.

So why do we do this? By feeding our inner self-talk we allow an on-going negative trajectory that works like a hamster wheel. It's only when we recognise this that we can start to mend ourselves. This is where a therapist can come in and reset this ingrained pattern.

Our re-programming should work like a meditation where we implement positive self-talk and affirmations. Start by saying this every morning: "Every day in every way, I'm getting better and better." This will lead to a feeling of "I can do it, I am strong enough, there are people who care about me, every day I get a little better." This mantra and a new list will be the first step towards healing emotionally. You will start feeling better and eventually positive about who you are. Bear in mind there are no quick fixes – re-programming the mind takes training and is relevant to people both behind and in front of The Wall.

NEGATIVE PROJECTIONS

An important consideration for the partner of a person who exists behind The Wall is how to avoid their negative projections and not replicate them.

A Recipient should ask themselves: "Can I let myself be who I am even when this person believes that I am responsible for how they feel?" and "Do I want to remain in a relationship with someone who sees me in a way that is out of alignment with who I know myself to be? And, if so, why?"

Not all of my clients have been part of a couple. Eva was a fitness instructor in her late thirties and was fascinated by the notion of the hidden world of emotions. She paid much attention to the concept of The Wall and noted that whilst some walls are obvious, others are more subtle.

"My mother exhibits some of the traits of a Wall Hider," she told me. "Often it's her way or no way. She's self-righteous to the end. She is aware of her behaviour but doesn't have the tools to control it. She automatically moves to blame. The result is that she pushes those people who are close to her, away, but this creates a void for her. All she has ever wanted is to be loved and accepted, but it seems that her mechanism of alienation keeps her connected to the pain she knew as a child. It makes me sad as I want to share things with her and be affectionate, but instead I stay away."

SETTING BOUNDARIES

Adelyn Birch says in her book – *Boundaries*:

After a Pathological Relationship

"A big part of confidence comes from setting boundaries, because they can make it possible to connect with others while maintaining your safety and your integrity,"

A GRANDMOTHER'S STORY:

A grandmother came to see me because her granddaughter of eighteen wanted to come and live with her. The girl had witnessed her parents' unhealthy marriage full of conflict and aggression and had been placed in the care of Social Services for three years. The grandmother didn't want to take on this burden but felt guilty because she felt an obligation to the girl.

The grandmother had finally reached an age where she was free to do all the things she's always hoped to. In the past she had always taken on the family problems and tried to make things better but now she was tired. I talked to her about setting boundaries but she didn't seem to understand what this meant or how to do it.

According to the grandmother, her son didn't like being asked direct questions, and I could tell from this that he was living behind The Wall. I told the grandmother that she had inadvertently taken away the responsibility of her son and grand-daughter to work out their own lives.

We discussed how implementing boundaries for both of them was something she should do out of love, not as a punishment, and that it was important for them to be accountable for their own decisions in life. The grandmother said she had never seen her behaviour in this way and would consider all we had talked about.

I didn't see her for a few weeks but when I did there was a noticeable change from the moment she entered the room. She sat down and immediately said: "I did it!"

She told me that her grand-daughter had found a family to stay with who were much closer in age. They were a family with another teenager, younger siblings with a mother whose main role was to look after the family. She went on to tell me that her grand-daughter had also found a place that takes in young people who self-harm and was already starting to feel better about herself.

However, the issue of her son came up again. She commented on the fact that he didn't respond to her and said this often caused her upset and pain. She told me he's always been like that and said she felt she never got anywhere with him, with all her attempts in the past ending up with her getting the blame. She said this made her feel helpless. She wondered whether she hadn't done enough for him when he was a child although he got as much care as her other children.

I showed her the image of The Wall and explained how the behaviour pattern of her son corresponded to it. She looked at it in silence for a while, then said: "Yes this is him!" The discovery seemed to come as a relief and she said, laughing: "This confirms things for me. I will pursue my own life from now on. I'm off on an adventure and to search for freedom!"

By becoming more self-aware we are on the right path to feeling and becoming empowered. In Daniel Goleman's book

Emotional Intelligence, he says: "If you lack self-awareness, if you are not able to manage your distressing emotions, if you can't have empathy and have effective relationships, then no matter how smart you are, you won't get very far."

Another writer, Travis Bradberry, says in his book *Emotional Intelligence 2.0*:

"A high degree of self-awareness requires a willingness to tolerate the discomfort of focusing on feelings that might be negative."

So, how can we benefit from developing more and higher self-awareness?

CHAPTER 9

The Path to Emotional Recovery

"When the wind of change rises we have two choices: we can build a wall or we can build a windmill."

Chinese Proverb.

DEVELOPING A HEALTHIER WALL

YOU MIGHT FIND YOURSELF questioning whether you have a Wall. You might wonder how you would recognise it. Would you need someone to point it out?

During my work it has become apparent that most people exhibit defence strategies to varying extents, although not many will have defences as pronounced as those of a Wall Hider.

For example, some people might be able to admit things and not be completely in denial, and instead of blaming they take responsibility and deal with their feelings.

Both The Wall Hider and his/her partner will need to put in work to make changes and get results. Perhaps surprisingly, that process is the same for both of them.

The best place to start is from the point of acceptance and forgiveness of yourself and your partner. In doing this your perspective widens and you will experience a paradigm shift of emotional awareness where realisation is needed in order to start changing emotional reactions. Some refer to this process as coming to your senses.

You start to see that you were powerless because you were trapped in old attitudes, belief systems and behavioural patterns. More importantly you were powerless over the other's behaviour. Once you realise this, you discover you can access the power to start changing your own behaviour. This will, in turn allow you to lead a more balanced life.

FACING YOUR EMOTIONAL SECRETS

When we embark on our spiritual path and move towards finding our authentic selves, we experience a transformation that happens from the inside out. This journey begins with the relationship we have with ourselves.

As Susie Orbach says in her series on Radio 3:

"One cannot discard one's past, like an unwanted coat. We have history, we come from somewhere, and we have attachments. Many are abused, ignored or hurt, and all those who might wish to flee and reinvent themselves, know they can only move forward with the acknowledgement of their past and what they've come from. Otherwise self-invention means dislocation from history and a deep dislocation from oneself. In striving to be the person that you want to be there may be enormous losses, fracturing and alienation. A crisis, often precipitated by loss compels them to seek the reflective space that therapy offers. As they try to find the words and feelings of what still hurts, the experience mutates. It doesn't disappear, but it sits inside them differently. The experience isn't split-off, disowned or repressed in a manner that is undermining – it becomes instead integrated. That ownership is, it constitutes change, it is not the kind of change that's about the dismissal or rejection of self, but a change that results of a kind of acceptance."

ACCEPTING UNPLEASANT AND UNCOMFORTABLE FEELINGS

At some point in life we have all experienced feelings that are unpleasant and uncomfortable like shame, guilt, fear of being left out or missing out, sadness, anger, jealousy, rivalry, envy and of course the most unpleasant and the one we try to avoid – often through a whole life – is Pain.

Our natural instinct is to shy away from them, deny them or ignore them. Often we reprimand ourselves by thinking we shouldn't feel that way or allow those thoughts. Instead, we would be better off acknowledging our feelings and accepting that it's normal to experience this range of emotions sometimes. The best way to manage these feelings it to acknowledge them and allow them to pass through us without fear.

Educator Palmer Parker said: "The human soul doesn't want

to be advised or fixed or saved. It simply wants to be witnessed exactly as it is."

LISA'S STORY:

> Working with my therapist over the past year has been a transformative experience. I approached her on the recommendation of a friend who had sought her counsel and clearly gained from the experience. I knew I needed help.

I told the therapist about my relationship and my partner's annoying behaviour. He always needed to be right! She showed me a design of what she called a defence wall, and she pointed at the bricks and explained how The Wall was supported by his behaviour. As I looked at The Wall, with its supporting beams/ behaviours, I felt like I was looking directly at my partner. It was as if the design had been based on him.

I made the decision that I had to bring the relationship to an end. I thought about all the pain I was experiencing every day and, metaphorically speaking, saw the writing on The Wall!

After having shared this with the therapist, we turned to explore emotions and feelings on a broader scale. We looked at how to handle and navigate the challenge of a new job in the City, with a tough boss and a feeling that I wasn't good enough.

She, the female boss seemed to react in the same way again and again when I made suggestions. She wouldn't hesitate to put me down in front of my colleagues, always made it clear that she was right and seemed incapable of ever being wrong. Her reaction caused me to worry, and I developed a blanket of guilt and shame that I would cower behind whenever she was around. I constantly questioned whether I was in the wrong, whether things were my fault; I blamed myself.

Then I remembered The Wall. My therapist reminded me: "It doesn't matter whether it's a partner or a boss, the emotional pattern that is built upon pride and the fear of being seen as weak is the same. And it results in the same toxic behaviour every time: passive aggression, controlling, criticism, anger and blame, which in turn creates confusion and weakness in others.

We worked to formulate strategies, both short and long term. I was surprised when one day she suggested that my boss might benefit from admitting instead of blame.

"Admitting?" I asked the therapist."

"Yes," she said.

"How can I admit anything to someone who has treated me like she has?

The therapist asked me how my boss made me feel. "It made me feel like I did when I was at school. I recall a trauma from my schooldays when my girlfriends suddenly changed and made me feel excluded from our usual group. This pain has followed me ever since."

During one of our sessions we had drawn a Neural Pathway sketch. This is a line that ends up in a square that shows where we keep historic feelings that remain with us since the trauma that caused them and we unfortunately seem to go back again and again and "visit" these unpleasant and can be detrimental old feelings and hurt. We recognize and understand where they stem from, we can start the healing process needed to erase them.

"Reflecting 12 months on, I'm not without challenges, but I have a whole new perspective on my past and present relationships. I can understand them better and not blame myself. My boss is no longer an issue, she's a friend. I have moved on from my past romantic relationship. As with everything, it's a constant work in progress. I've gained from the teachings of the therapist, and continue to work with her to use new tools and approaches for dealing with the inevitable curve balls life throws us."

USING ADMITTING

Lisa's female boss had a tendency to put her down, especially in front of other colleagues. Lisa dreaded going to work and became determined to find a way of moving out of her boss's grip.

We discussed how she might benefit from talking to her boss in a social gathering at work. This is what happened when she found the right moment to approach her and use admittance.

She said to her boss: "I admit I find it hurtful when you make unpleasant comments to me when we're in the middle of the office. I'm sure your intention isn't to hurt me, but unfortunately that's what happens." Her boss looked completely taken aback and said she had no idea her behaviour could be perceived like that! She said to Lisa: "Thank you for telling me this way. I will take it on as a good advice."

Lisa quickly saw results from their conversation. Her boss reacted differently to her. She was more attentive and relaxed and in the end the two of them developed a good connection.

CHAPTER 10

Your Life

SHALL I LEAVE OR SHALL I STAY?

WHEN A RELATIONSHIP IS inevitably lost, it's my job as the therapist to assist the breakup so that it happens in the most compassionate way, with each person being left with a sense of value. This enables the possibility of the couple communicating on a different level later, and can be achieved even in the most painful of negotiations, such as divorce.

It was encouraging to see how the wife of the first couple described their journey to recovery. She said she and her husband had gone through an emotional and spiritual transformation by using acceptance on many levels. She worked on finding a way to deal with her frustration by doing daily mindfulness-exercises, meditation and yoga, and continued seeing me, both on her own and also with her husband from time to time.

Acceptance is a powerful tool. The first thing to accept is that your partner could have a Wall in the first place. The second is that it may not be possible to change it.

Just because you may choose to accept something, doesn't mean that you need to like it. When you accept the way someone behaves or reacts you will feel empowered and able to find effective solutions.

WHAT'S NEXT?

One fact to be aware of is that it's unlikely that The Wall Hider will change unless they get to a point where they stand to lose something they don't want to lose.

Admitting is painful, but if you can incorporate this feeling into your situation, it will bring truth and understanding with it. If you can admit what is actually happening, you can accept it.

Once you get to this juncture, you can consider what to do. Do you stay in the relationship, or do you leave? Can you live with these behaviours? What in your own behaviour can you change so that you and your partner can move towards healing? What's at stake – children, money, property, memories, feelings that remain for one another in spite of you not being able to connect?

There is a reflection on acceptance in the book *Emotions Anonymous*:

> "Acceptance is hard to comprehend. I thought if I accepted something, that meant I liked it and I wanted it to stay. But this is not what acceptance is. Acceptance means being honest about what is happening in my life, what I am thinking, and what I am feeling. When I can

stop denying and rebelling against myself, I can relax and let go of the control. When I stop trying to control, I am open to the learning and healing which is waiting for me."

AMY'S STORY:

Recently I received my Decree Nisi. I felt as if, after five years of being put down and belittled constantly, I had lost all my strength and finally now, with the arrival of my Decree Nisi, I could celebrate. During my marriage, I was perpetually on the edge, as my husband was always controlling and on the verge of an outburst with my two young sons and me. He had no patience and, as a consequence, our young sons became nervous and insecure.

One day, an old friend who often came to visit, looked at me and said: "How much longer can you put up with this?" I was surprised and asked what he meant. He commented on the way my husband treated me and the boys.

The fact that he'd confirmed my own sentiments about the way my husband treated me and my children was a weight off my shoulders.

I knew, at that point, I needed to do something. He suggested I find a therapist which made sense to me. Fortunately, he knew of someone with a lot of experience working with victims of abuse, and from the first moment I met the counsellor, I felt understood.

In our relationship, my husband had often twisted things to make me feel weak and make me believe everything was my fault. After years of this I suffered from low self-esteem and sometimes extreme exhaustion. It was a relief to meet with someone who seems to understand his behaviours as if she knew him, and who was able to confirm his anger, dominance and control.

The counsellor was able to explain his behaviours in detail by showing me an image of The Wall. It made a lot of sense to me. The description of his defences made sense as I knew about his unfortunate childhood. The behaviour described how he always need to be right.

Once I was in possession of all the information, I had a moment of clarity. I decided I had to find a way out of the relationship. I had no idea how I would do this and worried whether we would have enough money to survive or whether he would sabotage me.

HOW DO WE GET THROUGH A BREAK-UP?

Re-programming the brain should work like a meditation where we repeatedly implement positive self-talk and affirmations. If you start with something like: "I might not be perfect, but I am good as I am," this will lead to a feeling of:

"I can do it."

"I am strong enough."

"There are people who care about me."

To aid recovery after a break up, ask yourself the following questions:

Am I able to allow my partner's negative projections to remain his own, or will I be impacted by them and eventually manifest them myself?

Can I truly be myself when my partner believes that I am

responsible for how he feels?

Do I want to remain in a relationship with someone who sees me in a way that is out of alignment with who I know myself to be?

REPLACING OUTDATED BEHAVIOURS

In order to replace outdated behaviours with improved ones, we need to be aware of our own weaknesses, and understand how they can leave us feeling vulnerable. This is crucial in the process of building healthy defence mechanisms to protect our own values and who we are at our core. As the recipient, you will wonder whether your partner, The Wall Hider, will be able to move beyond his preconditioned behaviours.

In the case of the earlier couple, it was the thought that he might lose his wife, that prompted the husband, The Wall Hider, to contemplate making any changes. I had indicated to them the importance of setting time aside to spend together, outside of their role as parents. The husband had ended up listening to his wife's emotional sharing, which he hadn't been able or willing to do for years.

The husband acknowledged this was the price for keeping the equilibrium of their marriage, and cared sufficiently for his wife to make the necessary changes. He realised that in coming to me with his wife for counselling sessions he had found the safety net he needed in which to understand, accept and modify his behaviours.

When we value ourselves, we feel able to define what it is we want in life and what we want from our relationships. Whilst setting boundaries will improve the recipient's quality of life, it will not magically erase outmoded behavioural patterns and old beliefs. A suitable therapist is essential if you are serious about working on yourself and your issues. He or she will help you to recognise, explore and reflect on past beliefs and weaknesses, and enable you to adopt new patterns and build better relationships.

By becoming more self-aware you will be on the right path to becoming empowered. You will, therefore, be more able to ask yourself whether you are able to understand and accept the way your partner is. Or whether you need someone who is more like you instead, who is able to share feelings and emotions, and who is responsive. To be "emotional" is not necessary the same as being able to express and share emotions.

How can we benefit from developing a higher self-awareness? *The Cambridge Dictionary* describes self-awareness as follows:

"Knowledge that something exists, or understanding of a situation or subject at the present, based on information or experience."

EMOTIONAL RECOVERY

A crisis, often triggered by a loss or a relationship stuck in blame and anger, compels people to seek the reflective space that therapy offers. As a person tries to find the words and feelings to describe their pain, the experience mutates. It doesn't disappear, but it sits inside the individual differently. The experience isn't split-off, disowned or repressed in a manner that is undermining. Instead it becomes a known entity and therefore integrated. That ownership of pain is transformative, as it constitutes change. Not the kind of change that's about the dismissal or rejection of self, but a change triggered by admittance.

This journey begins with the relationship we have with

96

ourselves. Looking inwardly, you might ask yourself whether you have any semblance of The Wall in your own life. You might question what it is that is stopping you from having healthy relationships and leading the life you deserve.

For someone hiding behind The Wall, it is possible that his/her Wall might mutate over time as the couple grow and develop greater insight into how The Family Map influences who they are today. In doing that, they can get to better know more about themselves and formulate strategies that will bring them towards healing and, where necessary, to building a healthier Wall.

EMOTIONAL AWARENESS TRAINING

Eckhart Tolle the spiritual teacher and the author of *The Power of Now*: "Awareness is the greatest agent for change." So, once you have opened for the value of awareness you might begin to notice what triggers your reactions. You might start to understand how you can stay centred when those situations arise, knowing that your partner will play out specific behaviours because that's his/her pattern. They won't even notice they're doing it. In a sense, the power of observation gives you the gift of self-mastery over the situation.

We all have patterns in the way we handle our emotions. We either "Act IN" by sulking, withdrawing, cancelling or by being passive aggressive. Or we "Act Out". When someone "Act OUT," we might see anger, violence, blame, humiliation, sarcasm etc. (See the illustration on the following page.)

"Acting ON" means to share emotions, own them, recognising the feeling, express them, and the very best then is to do this without any undertone or blame.

MINDFULLNESS AND MEDITATION

By practising mindfulness and meditation, we increase the ability to notice what's going on around us. We can observe ourselves. A good exercise is to imagine yourself sitting in a theatre and to watch yourself on the stage. You can enact your behaviour in challenging situations and see where and how you could have improved things.

When we sit back and watch what's going on, our power is able to flow through us, not from us. Our observations can help to empower us, making us less vulnerable and less at risk of being manipulated and being made to feel powerless by the person we are with.

Moving from Negative to Positive Handling of Emotions:		
Selfish and Self-Seeking	to	Interest in Others
Dishonest	to	Admittance/Honesty
Fear	to	Faith/Freedom
Pride	to	Humility
Withholding	to	Sharing Feelings

We can explore the effectiveness of The Wall as a concept using the outcomes from the couples we looked at in the book.

There is evidently a difference between the thickness and height of people's Walls, and there is also a difference in the recipients as characters with each having their own individual issues. But regardless of the specifics of each person and each relationship, we need to understand why someone has come to manifest their specific behaviours. We also need to ascertain how and whether we can accept these behaviours and find a way to cope with them. And it we can't, whether and how we leave the relationship.

CHAPTER 11

Resolutions

OUR FIRST COUPLE HAS continued to work on their relationship. The wife has started a teaching course and become stronger within herself, so doesn't need to rely on her husband for emotional fulfilment as much anymore. In turn the husband felt his wife to be less demanding and has been able to show more interest in her and behave with greater spontaneity.

John has found his vocation in the city he loves. He has a new flat and a new partner who is fun and creative. He sends me little greetings from time to time sharing news of his life.

Amy, who had decided to leave because she couldn't see any light ahead, is now divorced. Her husband did everything he could to make it difficult for her to leave him, but she got there in the end. She has found a job that suits her and is stronger and more able to cope with his recurring attempts to put her down or set obstacles before her and her sons.

Lisa found being alone led to a sense of freedom, which was the last thing she expected. She then met a new partner and they have since settled down together.

The Grandmother found a comfortable niche between her son and her grand-daughter, but maintained her goal of adventuring and living life to the full.

Emma, whose humour helped her through the tough times, was adamant that she would stay in her relationship for the duration of the time that the children needed her. She was the product of a broken family herself and felt the children needed the stability of two parents being together. She got involved in activities outside of her family to keep her busy and engaged as her husband often travelled abroad with work. She continued to come to sessions regularly, and would always leave questioning whether she could go back and face staying for another round.

Although we have examined heterosexual couples where The Wall Hiders happen to have been predominantly men, the patterns exist within women behind The Wall too, and I often see male clients who have been hurt and are in pain because the partner or wife can be vindictive and frequently takes it out on their rights to see the children. As with male Wall Hiders, these women's position behind The Wall stems from childhood trauma neglect or abuse.

Once we start our emotional recovery from old conditioning, we become aware of how certain events triggered certain behaviours and required coping strategies that are now outdated. Once we have established this, we can start by going through a process of acceptance and forgiveness of both oneself and others.

As our perspective widens and our experience grows it feels as though we are coming to our senses. This is a shift in our emotional awareness. It's at this point that we start realising what we need to do to start changing our emotional reactions and how we behave when doing that. We start to see why we were trapped in old attitudes, outdated belief systems and poor behavioural patterns.

From *Daily Reflections* by Hazelden Publishing:

The Partner Who Provided a Place to Climb to

Once when climbing rocks with friends, a woman reached a place she decided was impossible to move beyond. She wanted to retreat, but the leader encouraged her to try again. She felt angry and scared, and she was stuck. She fought with the rock, but it was clear that the rock was never going to budge. Wanting the rock to change shape or move was futile.

After she vented frustration at her situation, she realized there were only two ways out of her predicament. One was to quit, and the other was to try again, perhaps with a different mind-set than she had before. Proceeding with her task in spite of her fear, she began to think of the rock as her friend, as a partner who provided a place to climb. She realized that she did not have to make her friend, the rock, change in order to continue climbing. Her thoughts were more focused, and as a consequence she saw spaces and opportunities she wouldn't have otherwise noticed. Before she knew it, she found herself making her way up the rock.

Sometimes our partners can feel like an immovable rock. It's difficult to stop trying to change our partners and instead focus on ourselves. But when we do, we will discover a new direction in our relationship, a new view of our partner, and empowerment for ourselves.

SPACE FOR NOTES

HERE ARE SOME EMOTIONS YOU MAY BE FEELING. CIRCLE THOSE THAT APPLY, OR, FILL IN YOUR OWN EMOTIONS BELOW:

Peaceful	Optimistic	Joyful	Capable
Vulnerable	Liberated	Fulfilled	Jealous
Insecure	Inadequate	Frightened	Astonished
Eager	Amused	Confident	Courageous
Surprised	Irritated	Angry	Sad
Ashamed	Isolated	Resentful	Sceptical
Provoked	Worthless	Hurt	Aggressive
Guilty	Disappointed	Envious	Competitive
Choked	Rivalrous	Needy	Confused

SPACE FOR LISTING MORE OF YOUR OWN EMOTIONS AND FEELINGS:

SPACE FOR LISTING THE OTHER PERSON'S ROLE IN THE EVENTUAL CONFLICT:

SPACE FOR LISTING MY ROLE IN AN EVENTUAL CONFLICT:

SPACE FOR LISTING WHERE WE MIGHT BE IN THE WRONG:

SPACE FOR EXPLORING WHERE WE CAN USE ADMITTING:

SPACE FOR LISTING THINGS TO BE GRATEFUL FOR:

CREATE YOUR OWN FAMILY MAP:

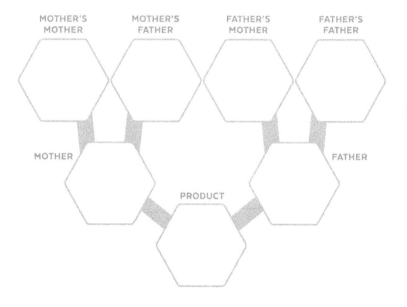

LIST HOW YOUR OWN EMOTIONS ARE EITHER ACTED **IN, ON,** OR **OUT:**

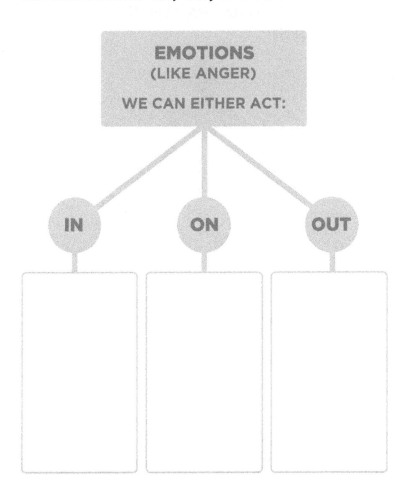

FILL OUT YOUR OWN BEHAVIOUR (DEFENCE MECHANISMS AND, EVENTUALLY, YOUR PARTNER'S OR OTHER'S):

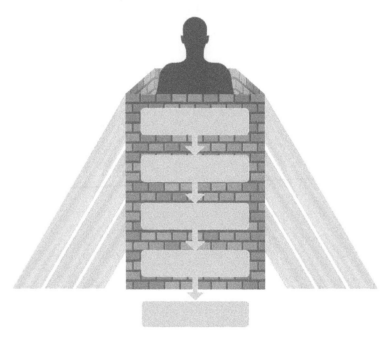

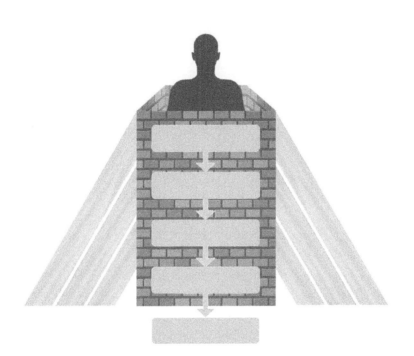